THE COUNTRY DOCTOR

for my parents

Ivan Turgenev

THE COUNTRY DOCTOR

Adapted for the stage by

Simon Day

OBERON BOOKS

LONDON

First published in this adaptation in 2002 by Oberon Books Ltd. (incorporating Absolute Classics)
521 Caledonian Road, London N7 9RH
Tel: 020 7607 3637 / Fax: 020 7607 3629
e-mail: oberon.books@btinternet.com
www.oberonbooks.com

A catalogue record for this book is available from the British Library.

ISBN: 1 84002 351 1

Cover design: Andrzej Klimowski

Characters

DOCTOR

TURGENEV

LANDLADY

MAID

MOTHER

ALEXANDRA

The play should be performed by four actors, the two women doubling.

This adaptation of *The Country Doctor* was first performed at The National Theatre (Olivier) on 29 October 2002, with the following cast:

DOCTOR, Richard Hollis

TURGENEV, Thomas Arnold

LANDLADY/MOTHER, Janet Spencer-Turner

MAID/ALEXANDRA, Jennifer Scott-Malden

Director, Katie Read

Designer, Miranda Nolan

Music, Richard Blair-Oliphant

with special thanks to Jack Bradley and Angus Mackechnie

Scene 1

Rural Russia, late 1830s. A room in a country inn. The DOCTOR, mid-thirties, shabbily dressed and holding a large medical bag, stands and looks at the motionless figure of a young Ivan TURGENEV, who lies on a chaise with his back to the audience.

DOCTOR: Fine, thanks for asking. No distance. A mile at the most. The bag? Light as a feather. Even with all the glass bottles, the solid brass instruments. And the roads are so well maintained in Oryol province, it's a joy to walk anywhere. Especially for a man with an ingrowing toenail. Whoever said walking is good for you? It may lengthen your life, but that's not the same thing as being good for you. Life's painful enough. I prescribe instant pleasure. Such as unadulterated birch snuff.

He takes two hefty pinches of snuff. His voice becomes strained and shrill. He sits. His feet are evidently causing him great pain.

If the government gave us our own coach and pair we wouldn't have to rely on a patient deigning to send a carriage. If indeed he does deign. Of course, it is a handy clue as to your possible earnings. If the coachman smiles at you, doffs his cap, your heart sinks – you think, oh bugger, *you're* not employed by anyone of means, but when he hardly acknowledges you, when he mutters 'get in' like he's talking to a dog, then you know you'll come away with a ten rouble note and several warm brandies in your stomach. Well, your clothes are nicely tailored. If we were paid properly, by the government – we are safeguarding the health of the country after all – then we wouldn't have to suffer this ignominy. We could turn a job down if we felt like it. People would swiftly learn they can't go falling ill whenever it damn well pleases them. If I were the Tsar, I'd make sure all doctors were paid…no, if I were the Tsar, I'd tell the doctors to go hang themselves, the snivelling lowlife.

The LANDLADY enters. She carries a bowl of hot water and towels.

LANDLADY: Still asleep?

DOCTOR: Dead to the world.

LANDLADY: What do you think?

DOCTOR: I haven't yet commenced my examination.

LANDLADY: You don't need to. He's caught a fever.

DOCTOR: He's caught a chill, from which a fever appears to have developed. Shooting woodcock. Why else would a gentleman go out to the birch forests in the early hours and lie around in the wet grass? We doctors are trained to look for clues: notice the damp breeches and the sliver of birch bark caught in his bootstrap.

LANDLADY: There's also a gun and a brace of woodcock on the table.

DOCTOR: If you wouldn't mind bringing some tea.

LANDLADY: He'll only slop it.

DOCTOR: For me.

He takes the bowl from her.

LANDLADY: How's your wife?

DOCTOR: Fine. Couldn't be better.

LANDLADY: I'd give him a sudorific and apply a mustard-plaster. But you're the doctor.

He pulls off his boots.

My husband's still the low-down, time-wasting good-for-nothing that he always was.

DOCTOR: Oh dear.

He takes off his socks.

LANDLADY: Still the drunk. The bully. Still got a mouth on him – fouler than an army shithouse.

He immerses his feet in the hot water.

I thought you wanted that for him. I know why they do it. Shoot. All men, not just the toffs. Because they can't appreciate a thing unless they bring it down. This one's a writer. Mother's the richest woman this side of Moscow. He said he was out hunting. Birds, said I – stories, said he. And then he collapses in that chair. There you are again, the writers – all men.

DOCTOR: Well, in fact there have been a few…

LANDLADY: Not happy knowing there's all these stories flying around. They have to shoot them down, stick their names on them – their scent. Filthy, murderous foxes with their terrible, stinking piss they spray on everything.

DOCTOR: About that tea.

LANDLADY: It's all to do with babies. It cripples them. That we can and they can't. After all, what difference are they making to the world? So they maim and they murder instead. How many women murderers have you known?

DOCTOR: Again, I think there have been…

LANDLADY: Not in our nature. We're much happier in ourselves.

DOCTOR: (*Indicating TURGENEV, who is stirring.*) I think…

He quickly towels his feet and stands up. She lingers.

LANDLADY: Oh, well yes, there's her. But I've got my theories about her.

DOCTOR: Eh?

LANDLADY: It's not right to gossip, doctor. I'm surprised at you. But yes, heartless bitch. I don't if she's actually, you know…whipping, yes, and it was rumoured she shot one of her serfs in the leg, but as for full-blown…then again, if my theory's correct: see, she never lets anyone get within five yards. Rides down from Spasskoye in a closed carriage. But once or twice I've caught sight of her old face – caked with paint and powder. To hide the lines? No. To hide the beard.

DOCTOR: Beard?

LANDLADY: Stubble. Thick, mannish. Freak of nature. So maybe you're right about the murdering. Shhh.

DOCTOR: Right. Let's have a look at you then, shall we?

Lights fade.

Scene 2

Lights up on the same scene, minutes later. The LANDLADY has left and the DOCTOR is putting away his medical kit.

DOCTOR: I insist, no talking. What you need is rest. Silence and stillness will cure any illness. I recommend you stay here at least until tomorrow morning. Word can be sent to your mother. Your beater has a cart, I suppose? Just nod. Well, I'll tell him to set off for Spasskoye. I care, you see. You don't get that with your city doctors. These boots bite like ferrets. I must get new ones. But they're so blessed expensive. So you're a writer, then? Nod, please. Silence and stillness. Had anything published? Well, I'm sure it'll come. I've often thought about turning my hand to writing. It's been commented that I have a certain way with words. On occasions I have even received something extra, you know, in consideration of…bedside manner – an ability to cheer up the patient – with stories…received an extra…how low is a man expected to stoop?

Tea is brought in by a MAID in a dirty apron.

MAID: Tea. Well?

DOCTOR: Thank you.

MAID: No.

DOCTOR: What?

MAID: Forty kopeks. Twenty for the tea and twenty for the service. You ordered it.

The DOCTOR looks at TURGENEV, but it is in vain. Exasperated, he reaches for some coins.

DOCTOR: He's ill.

MAID: We all die in the end.

She leaves.

DOCTOR: (*Calling.*) Aren't you going to pour it? Such vulgarity. Asking like that. Milk? Yes, I've come across some stories in my time. The things people tell you when they think they're on the brink of…it's like we're all imprisoned. I've had fantasies of being the man I'd be if I was on the point of snuffing it. You could tell all those petty, pocket-raiding tax-collector arse-wipes to go and jump off a cliff. Or if your wife was chewing your ears, you could say, 'Shut it, you dreadful hag.' If you felt the urge, you could run stark naked through the street. And no one would dare say a thing. 'Poor chap's dying,' they'd think. Then there's all the other stuff. You could take the gamble. What gamble? You'd be dead soon! 'I love you!' you'd suddenly say. 'My heart sings with the sound of your name! I'll lay down my whole life for you!' Of course you'd have to feel it in the first place. Most people don't have anyone to…for most people it would be the running naked.

A scream. The LANDLADY drags the MAID in by her ear.

LANDLADY: Go on.

MAID: Sorry.

LANDLADY: Mean it.

MAID: Sorry!

LANDLADY: And?

MAID: Here.

She gives a coin back to the doctor.

LANDLADY: Both.

MAID: But I…

LANDLADY: Both!

MAID: I carried it! I deserve…

LANDLADY: A good thrashing. Now give!

MAID: It's not fair.

She throws the other coin down.

LANDLADY: Pick that up!

The MAID exits weeping. The LANDLADY picks up the coins.

She's not all there. I blame the parents. Well, one of them. The father – peasant stock. She's inherited his moronic nature.

DOCTOR: Where did you find her?

LANDLADY: Between my legs, screaming, eighteen years ago. She's been screaming ever since. Tea's on the house.

She leaves.

DOCTOR: Well, I'll be off. I have a number of other calls.

She re-enters.

LANDLADY: I know what you're thinking but she's given us a lot of trouble and I've tried my best with no help from him and I know I drive him away with all my...and yes, we can at least take you in and give you a cup of tea but maybe in return you could spare a tiny thought for those of us who are really struggling and find something in that sodding bag of yours – something for the nagging in my head, it's like a woodpecker, and while you're at it something for him, too...he hasn't touched me for years...something to give his pride a bit of a lift. I'm sorry.

She goes. He picks up his bag and opens it.

DOCTOR: You don't need to be on the brink of death to be on the brink. Sometimes I wish I worked in a quarry. All alone with lumps of stone.

The LANDLADY re-enters.

LANDLADY: I've remembered why I... (*Addressing TURGENEV.*) If ever a position were to come up, sir, at your mother's estate – she's a good seamstress. Polite. Dependable. Sunny nature. And by God is she amenable. Strong thumbs. Strong wrists.

DOCTOR: Please...

LANDLADY: Well, I've sown the seed. Think it over.

DOCTOR: For you.

He gives her a little bottle.

13

For him.

He gives her a second bottle. She leaves again. TURGENEV takes some coins from his pocket.

What's that? Oh, that's too much. Please, I can't possibly accept. Well, I could, but only with reluctance, which I am prepared to do. Thank you. You observe how these financial matters erode my soul? I should see a doctor. Thank you.

He stretches out his hand to receive the money. Lights fade.

Scene 3

Lights up on the same. The DOCTOR has removed his coat and is seated at a small table. He is holding some playing cards. He turns them slowly. They are all picture cards. TURGENEV lets his hand fall to the floor. The DOCTOR laughs and picks up TURGENEV's cards.

DOCTOR: I bet you're relieved we only played for kopek stakes. I'm glad I stayed. Look at me, kicking a man when he's down. If I were a true Hippocrat, I'd have let you walk all over me. Nothing like a victory for giving the body a boost. I feel wonderful. No, but it was obvious that I am a seasoned player, that I am going to win, and the last thing an ailing man needs is to be patronised. Better to have an honest-to-God fleecing and be done with it. I don't feel bad about those other calls. Sod them. What's the point in being called a patient if you're not prepared to wait?

He takes some snuff.

It's rare that one gets a chance to talk to a man with wider horizons. Something happened to…someone I once…no, never mind.

Pause.

What are you writing about at the moment? Let me guess. Your mother. Writers love writing about their mothers. By immortalising them the sons feel they're repaying a debt, I suppose. No?

TURGENEV points weakly.

What? The gun? Don't speak. Hunting. You're writing about hunting. Yes, but there's more. You go hunting because you don't want to be anywhere near your mother? Right! When you look down the barrel you don't see a woodcock, you see your mother. Ha! Wait a minute…sick…vomit…you feel so guilty for having those thoughts that it makes you physically ill? How interesting. Oh, I see, you're actually…here.

He picks up the bowl and rushes forward. TURGENEV retches.

I'll call by tomorrow. You'll have a dreadful night, drowning in the boiling sea of your own sweat, but in the morning you'll reach dry land. Remember: silence and stillness.

Pause.

I nearly told you a story. But such a betrayal might…for those involved…anyway, you'd only take it and twist it all about, or you might not do anything with it. I can't write it. Can't get enough distance. These things are better left untold.

Pause.

Goodbye then.

He turns to go and almost instantaneously spins round, removing his coat and letting it fall to the floor. The floodgates have opened.

It was in Lent – when good Christians give things up – at the time of the thaw, and I was sitting with our local judge, Pavel Lukich Mylov – do you know him? – anyway, we were playing a hand of Preference, when a coachman arrives with a note. It's from a landowner's widow. For widow read penniless. 'My daughter's dying,' it says, 'For God's sake come. I've sent horses to fetch you.' I look out of the window. Sure enough, a miserable cart drawn by two pot-bellied nags, just my luck, and it's a filthy old night, but I can't refuse, not in front of the judge. The journey was hell: melting snow, rivers of mud, trees fallen over the road, and then suddenly a burst dam! The cart nearly capsizes, not that I'd have been any less comfortable if it had, and then the two clapped-out nags develop raging flatulence, of which I am downwind, so I arrive sodden, asphyxiated, not to say marinated, at this little thatched house in the middle of absolutely nowhere. Why does this bloody country have to be so big? And I'm standing there, cursing the roads, and the weather, when the door opens.

The actress playing the LANDLADY now appears as this new character, the MOTHER, dressed all in black and with a cap on her head.

MOTHER: Doctor.

DOCTOR: A pretty woman with sad eyes.

MOTHER: Save her, she is dying.

DOCTOR: I wish you could see her. Her bravery melted one's heart, almost enough to make one forget one's journey.

MOTHER: Please.

DOCTOR: Hers was a soul in torment. A child should never die before its parent.

MOTHER: I beg you, doctor, hurry.

DOCTOR: (*To the MOTHER.*) Where is the patient?

MOTHER: Come this way.

DOCTOR: I am led into the house and along a corridor to a small bedroom.

MOTHER: In here.

DOCTOR: Wait. Tell me about her.

MOTHER: She's my only child. She was the apple of her father's eye, the peach, the pomegranate. Even she couldn't keep him alive. And now the fever's taking her. Yesterday she was in perfect health, by lunchtime today she had a headache, and now she's dying of the plague.

DOCTOR: Well, we don't know…

MOTHER: She's all I've got. She's my every star, my moon, my wind, my food. She was born to live a long and happy life. A charmed, rainbow-coloured life. She's only twenty. She brings joy to all who meet her. Please, doctor. Save my Alexandra.

DOCTOR: And so I went in. And there she was. Alexandra Andreyevna. If only words had the potency to conjure up her face for you.

We now see the actress who played the MAID reappear as this new character, ALEXANDRA. She lies unconscious in a bed, breathing heavily. Her fever is dangerously high.

MOTHER: Doctor?

DOCTOR: I look at her.

MOTHER: Doctor?

DOCTOR: I cannot take my eyes off her.

MOTHER: What is it?

DOCTOR: I'm transfixed.

MOTHER: Is she beyond hope?

DOCTOR: I have never seen anyone look…

MOTHER: So ill? Oh God.

DOCTOR: So beautiful. Her every feature. Perfection. Absolutely exquisite. Quite the loveliest face I'd ever seen.

MOTHER: What?

DOCTOR: Nothing.

MOTHER: Is there any hope at all? I have to know!

DOCTOR: The mother was plainly desperate. I saw that my first duty was to pacify her. This was a highly delicate situation. We doctors pride ourselves on our ability to choose our words as we would choose our medicines. I thought long and hard. (*To the MOTHER.*) Calm down, woman. (*To TURGENEV.*) That seemed to do the trick.

MOTHER: (*Hysterical.*) How am I supposed to calm down? This is my only child! You have to tell me what's wrong with her!

ALEXANDRA thrashes about, calling out unintelligibly.

DOCTOR: (*To the MOTHER, impatiently.*) You've woken her. Your distress will only add to that of the patient's. Perhaps I might be left alone with her? (*To TURGENEV.*) But she wouldn't go, so I set to work. I bleed her, I apply several mustard plasters, I prepare and administer certain compounds, medicines, unguents. I am so close to her wonderful face. At last, things settle, the storm passes, and she begins to sweat. She partly recovers consciousness. (*To the MOTHER.*) There.

The girl opens her eyes, smiles, and passes her hand over her face.

MOTHER: What is it?

DOCTOR: Shhh.

MOTHER: What's the matter my darling?

ALEXANDRA: Nothing.

She turns her head away.

Nothing.

MOTHER: Doctor?

DOCTOR: We must leave her in peace. She needs to sleep.

MOTHER: Will you please stay the night?

DOCTOR: (*To TURGENEV.*) Well, I wasn't going to get back in that horse-drawn boat! (*To the MOTHER.*) I have several other calls to make.

MOTHER: The samovar's full, and there's rum in the parlour.

DOCTOR: (*To TURGENEV.*) I wouldn't have left that house if the Tsar himself had commanded me. (*To the MOTHER.*) Madam, other people are in dire need of my help.

MOTHER: A pitcher of rum and a ten rouble note.

DOCTOR: Well...

MOTHER: Fifteen roubles.

DOCTOR: (*To TURGENEV.*) But a man's got to live. (*To the MOTHER.*) Show me to my room, madam. (*To TURGENEV.*) A bed was made up for me in the drawing room.

MOTHER: Goodnight, doctor. Please feel free to read any of my husband's books.

DOCTOR: (*To TURGENEV.*) I lay down, but couldn't get to sleep. The drawing room was next to Alexandra's bedroom. Her head was this far away from mine, separated only by a wall. I lay there, in a state of deep distraction. Her face was everywhere. Hundreds of Alexandras, like golden icons, demure, virginal, pictures of pure and perfect light, floating around above my pillow. Those eyes. Alexandra was inside my head. God, what was I doing? I had allowed my personal desires to interfere with my professional obligations. I had to be strong. I was here in a medical capacity. So I decided…to go and check on my patient. I went to her room. My heart was thumping. I opened the door. Only to behold…

The MOTHER is sitting on a chair at the foot of the daughter's bed.

The mother bear, guarding her young. But the day had been a long one for her.

Her head drops onto her chest. The doctor tiptoes past her.

I felt like Perseus, stealing past the many-eyed Cetus to get to Andromache…or was it Andromeda? No, she was no monster, and what was I doing? The girl was asleep. Silence and stillness, remember? But her face drew me to it. I wanted to steal her. We'd gallop away, up into the night skies on the silver wings of Pegasus.

ALEXANDRA: Who are you?

DOCTOR: Don't be afraid. I am…the doctor. Your mother sent for me. I've given you medicines, and now you must rest, and in two days, with God's help, we'll have you up and about.

ALEXANDRA: Oh, yes. Yes, doctor, don't let me die. Please!

DOCTOR: Don't be silly. Who said anything about dying?

ALEXANDRA: I don't want to die, doctor.

DOCTOR: Now shhhh. Your mother!

She grabs his hand.

ALEXANDRA: I'll tell you why I don't want to die. Do you want to know? I'll tell you, doctor. But not a word to anyone. Come close.

DOCTOR: (*To TURGENEV.*) I obeyed.

ALEXANDRA: Closer.

DOCTOR: Her lips brushed my ear. Her hair touched my cheek. My head was spinning.

She whispers for a long time in his ear. Finally he stands up.

ALEXANDRA: Remember, not a word.

He nods solemnly and draws back from the bed. She falls asleep.

DOCTOR: (*To TURGENEV.*) Of course you'll want to know what she whispered. And of course you won't believe me when I tell you it was utter gobbledygook, could have been ancient Greek. Don't smile. She was delirious. Look, why would I lie to you? Why would I sully the...never mind. Shall I carry on? I'll take that as a yes.

He gets out his snuff pouch and takes two hefty pinches.

Well, the next day she was no better. And the thaw got worse, so leaving wasn't an option. After a few days I felt as if I'd been there for months.

MOTHER: Soup, doctor?

DOCTOR: It was like I was part of the family.

MOTHER: My husband loved soup. We never lived high on the hog. He was the best man I ever knew. He didn't approve of extravagant living, not that that was even on the menu, we were never well off – he was a scholar, an academic. His wealth was of principles. He believed in his country. He hated greed and selfishness.

DOCTOR: Quite right.

MOTHER: His duty, as he saw it, was to plough as much as he could back into the land. To pay his taxes. To educate his daughter. We lived on books and soup.

DOCTOR: Very good it is, too.

MOTHER: His spirit lives on. In the beets, the potatoes. In the cabbages. You can taste it.

DOCTOR: Yes.

MOTHER: We've always given our surplus crop to the poor.

DOCTOR: How inspiring.

MOTHER: A drop more?

DOCTOR: Thank you.

MOTHER: He would have liked you. He would have appreciated your selflessness. He's out there now, watching over us. Watching you nurse his beloved Alexandra back to health. I'm so happy, now she is beginning to show signs of recovery.

DOCTOR: (*To TURGENEV.*) Where did she get that idea?

MOTHER: You did say so, didn't you?

DOCTOR: Yes, of course. (*To TURGENEV.*) I had no choice!

MOTHER: Thank God. You're a good man, doctor.

DOCTOR: She'd put her faith in me – and her blasted husband's! In any case, a positive attitude is crucial to convalescence. We all of us underestimate the power of

the mind with regard to illness. (*To the MOTHER.*) She's
going to be fine. (*To TURGENEV.*) I needed to buy
myself some time. I banned her from Alexandra's
bedroom and I myself kept vigil around the clock. I
scoured the pages of my medical books, not forgetting to
keep a sharp eye on the patient herself. I loved to watch
her face as she slept – silence and stillness – but it was
sheer agony not to hear her voice. Agony. Enough to
make you...cough.

*He coughs violently, and looks to ALEXANDRA, who sleeps
on.*

Or affect your balance.

He 'accidentally' knocks a vase off a table. She sleeps on.

Or make you suddenly exclaim: 'What am I to do? God
help me! Aaaargh! Wake up!'

She wakes.

Oh, Alexandra, you must try and sleep. (*To
TURGENEV.*) I couldn't help myself. (*To ALEXANDRA.*)
You're hot. Let me rub some cool ointment on your
hands.

ALEXANDRA: Tell me a story.

DOCTOR: No. Oh very well.

MOTHER: Doctor.

DOCTOR: Just a moment, Alexandra. (*To TURGENEV.*)
Why would she not leave us alone?

MOTHER: I don't understand, doctor. If she's getting
better, then surely it won't hurt for me to see her.

DOCTOR: Are you questioning my medical probity?

MOTHER: No, but...

DOCTOR: I need to be absolutely sure that whatever was wrong with her has been eradicated. A relapse at this stage might prove fatal. (*To TURGENEV.*) She finally left us in peace, knocking only to alert us to the tray of soup outside the door.

He attempts to feed ALEXANDRA a spoonful of soup.

You really must try.

ALEXANDRA: It'll only come up again, like yesterday.

DOCTOR: (*To TURGENEV.*) She was dangerously weak.

ALEXANDRA: Talk to me, doctor.

DOCTOR: You should sleep.

ALEXANDRA: I love the sound of your voice.

DOCTOR: Oh, now!

ALEXANDRA: It soothes me. More than all those medicines put together. Tell me something.

DOCTOR: What?

ALEXANDRA: Tell me about yourself. Your life. Put me into a coma. I'm teasing. Your student days. Were you in St Petersburg or Moscow? Was your father a doctor too? Do you have brothers and sisters? Please talk to me.

DOCTOR: (*To TURGENEV.*) I wanted to lie. I wanted to credit myself with a noble lineage, elevate myself in her beautiful eyes. But they drew out the truth like the moon draws the tides. (*To ALEXANDRA.*) Where shall I begin?

ALEXANDRA: Begin with…love. Don't be embarrassed.

DOCTOR: I'm not! It's just that there's no time for such things. A doctor's life is so absurdly busy. How about a nice game of cards?

ALEXANDRA: Are you married? No.

DOCTOR: How do you know?

ALEXANDRA: Well, are you?

DOCTOR: No.

ALEXANDRA: Have you ever kissed a girl?

DOCTOR: (*To TURGENEV.*) I don't need to tell you all the boring details, but suffice it to say that after a week had elapsed, a week of days and a week of nights, she and I had got to know one another intimately. We had read each other from cover to cover. To be known felt such a relief. She accepted me for what I was. (*To ALEXANDRA.*) Sing that song again.

ALEXANDRA: I feel weary.

DOCTOR: Yes, of course.

ALEXANDRA: Oh, you look so sad. Very well. (*She sings.*) 'As autumn came and the leaves turned brown, she wept full sore and her eyes looked down, for she knew the new buds she never would see, and she lay herself down at the roots of the evergreen tree.' You now.

DOCTOR: (*Sings.*) 'He found her lain by the evergreen tree, and a prettier bud he never did see, so he made the fair maid a thistledown gown, and he placed in her hair gold leaves that would do for a crown.'

ALEXANDRA/DOCTOR: (*Singing together.*) 'And as he crowned her, so it turned to spring, and they ran through the woods, the evergreen queen and king.'

DOCTOR: I feel...

ALEXANDRA: What? What is it that you feel?

DOCTOR: Happy.

ALEXANDRA: So do I. Deliriously.

MOTHER: Doctor?

DOCTOR: (*To TURGENEV.*) But there were still the occasional knockings at the door, the hushed inquiries. How could I tell her the truth?

ALEXANDRA: I don't want to see anyone but you.

DOCTOR: (*To the MOTHER.*) She's sleeping. (*To TURGENEV.*) What a lie! When had she last had a proper sleep?

ALEXANDRA: Tell her, doctor.

DOCTOR: I'm very pleased with the progress she's making.

ALEXANDRA: No one but you. No one.

MOTHER: But what am I to think, doctor? The coachman's just waded in from town with another box.

DOCTOR: I've got things in hand, madam. Trust me!

MOTHER: It's a large one. The seventh box in as many days.

DOCTOR: Well, could I have it please?

MOTHER: Why do you need it?

DOCTOR: I just do.

MOTHER: What's in it?

DOCTOR: Things.

MOTHER: Things?

DOCTOR: Private things.

MOTHER: Such as?

DOCTOR: Some tobacco. A razor. Four pairs of clean socks.

MOTHER: It's very heavy.

DOCTOR: And a brass astrolabe. I'm a fitful sleeper. I like to study the heavens.

MOTHER: Don't lie to me, doctor. The box is full of medicines.

DOCTOR: You opened it.

MOTHER: I had to.

DOCTOR: You opened my box. How dare...!

MOTHER: I needed to know.

DOCTOR: My private...!

MOTHER: She's my daughter! I have a right to know!

DOCTOR: Trust me. I am the doctor!

MOTHER: And I want to know how you can say she's getting better when every day another box of medicines arrives! Powders, pills, bottles, ointments – she's either got every single illness known to man, or you're in there clutching at straws!

ALEXANDRA: Make her go away!

MOTHER: Alexandra!

ALEXANDRA: Go away!

MOTHER: Please, doctor!

DOCTOR: You're upsetting her.

ALEXANDRA: GO AWAY!

DOCTOR: If you care about your daughter, you'll bring me my box immediately, and leave us both in peace!

MOTHER: Her precious life is in your hands!

DOCTOR: (*To TURGENEV.*) As if I didn't know that. A drowning man clutching at straws. Drowning in the dark

and fathomless sea of his own ineptitude. She was right.
There were empty jars and bottles everywhere. Medical
books lying open. Piles of case notes strewn across the
floor. You are not a doctor. You create characters, breathe
life into them until it's time, thematically, for them to
die. We deal with real human lives, and people forget
what an appalling responsibility that is – the pressure
you're under to diagnose with speed, to prescribe the
right treatment – and it's all right if you're one of those
hard-hearted bastards with their Moscow consulting
rooms, when it's only the money you're after – but I
have the great misfortune to care about my patients – in
this case care deeply – hell, I was madly in love with
Alexandra Andreyevna, and she was going to die so why
would I not panic! Why would I wait patiently to see if
the effects of one stupid random treatment worked or
not? Try this, you think. Or this. Or how about this!
Why not this and this! Why not all of them? And
suddenly you're Doctor Scattergun blasting at swifts.
And the sound of the gun drowns out the tiny voice of
conscience that's saying, 'Send for another doctor. Get a
second opinion.' It'd take days for them to get here, and
what if they saw the mistakes you'd made – fatal errors –
I'm not mending shoes – you'd get struck off, made to
look an abject fool by some little prick straight out of
medical school. No, you have to stick to your…
scatterguns.

ALEXANDRA: Doctor?

DOCTOR: I thought you were asleep.

ALEXANDRA: I was.

DOCTOR: What woke you? A bad dream?

ALEXANDRA: No. You were talking. Is everything all
    right?

DOCTOR: Everything's fine.

ALEXANDRA: You must ask my mother for more rum.

DOCTOR: Ah.

ALEXANDRA: And I'll lend you my hairbrush. If you think it's important to carry on pretending.

DOCTOR: I don't know what you...

ALEXANDRA: That you are not at the end of your tether. Come and sit with me. Let me tame your wild, wild hair.

She strokes his hair, which has indeed become wild.

Tell me then. Tell me how I'm nearly better. Tell me.

DOCTOR: You know I can't.

ALEXANDRA: Then tell me I'm going to die.

DOCTOR: No.

ALEXANDRA: Tell me.

DOCTOR: But why?

ALEXANDRA: Because it would be easier if I knew.

DOCTOR: What would?

ALEXANDRA: Tell me!

DOCTOR: But I don't know. I don't know anything for sure.

ALEXANDRA: You know one thing.

DOCTOR: What? What do I know?

ALEXANDRA: That you love me. Don't you?

DOCTOR: Yes. (*To TURGENEV.*) I'd said it. And now I'd said it there was nothing stopping me from feeling it. My heart unfolded. It felt as wide as the Caucasus, deeper than the Baltic. Yes, I loved her. I loved Alexandra Andreyevna, and now she knew it!

MOTHER: Doctor?

DOCTOR: Oh, Jesus Christ!

MOTHER: I need to talk to you.

DOCTOR: Wait, Alexandra.

ALEXANDRA: I'm feeling so sleepy.

DOCTOR: I won't be a second. (*To TURGENEV.*) I wanted to fling the door wide open, grab that interfering old hag by the throat and hurl her into the nearest ravine to be swept away by the floods. No, what I wanted to say was: (*To the MOTHER.*) Your daughter and I have fallen in love. Please send for a priest as we intend to be married. Any delay might jeopardise your chances of staying on here as scullery-maid and laundress. So look sharp. (*To TURGENEV.*) But I didn't open my mouth. She was looking at me with such tenderness and humility.

MOTHER: I believe in a God, doctor. There are so many reasons not to, but I cannot help myself. If Alexandra is dying, I would like to send for a priest.

DOCTOR: (*To TURGENEV.*) Yes, send for him! Send for the priest!

MOTHER: Shall I? Think of her soul, doctor. Don't send that beautiful soul to damnation. You're a good man. I know that. I can see it in your eyes. My husband would have liked you so much.

DOCTOR: (*To TURGENEV.*) Of course he would!

MOTHER: Can I send for the priest?

DOCTOR: (*To TURGENEV.*) What about *my* soul – I was in torment! I felt like I'd been let into a paradise where all the trees were dying and the longer I tried to stay there the more everything green and lush rotted and withered, including my soul – turned to ash, hot and blackened and abominated. What was I to do?

MOTHER: Can I?

DOCTOR: I wanted to close the door in her face. Why is a doctor never allowed to say 'I don't know'?

MOTHER: Doctor?

DOCTOR: 'I prevaricate. I equivocate. I vacillate.'

MOTHER: Please?

DOCTOR: If I kept thinking of the wedding, it might help. So I did. I imagined her in her snowy white dress, with blossoms cascading in a creamy soft rain upon our heads, and all presided over by a divine beneficence. And that wondrous image sustained me, helped me form the words, as I leant forward and, with tears in my eyes, said (*To the MOTHER.*) Yes. Send for the priest!

MOTHER: Thank you. Now everything is clear.

DOCTOR: (*To TURGENEV.*) I turned and went to the bed. I had to know. I had to ask her. Do you see? (*To ALEXANDRA.*) Alexandra? (*To TURGENEV.*) Silence and stillness. (*To ALEXANDRA.*) Alexandra Andreyevna! (*To TURGENEV.*) Was I too late?

He knocks a dish onto the floor with a clatter. She sits bolt upright, her lips parted, her eyes staring wildly.

Sorry, I'm so clumsy…

ALEXANDRA: Am I going to die? You have to tell me. Now!

DOCTOR: For heaven's sake.

ALEXANDRA: Tell me! Please tell me I'm not going to live.

DOCTOR: What?

ALEXANDRA: I have to know.

DOCTOR: Alexandra…

ALEXANDRA: No! You don't understand. If I can know for sure that I'm going to die, then I can say to you what I need to say to you. I implore you by everything that's holy. Nothing in the world matters to me as much as this. Please. For the love of God.

DOCTOR: (*To TURGENEV.*) Could it be what I had hoped for? I had to know. (*To ALEXANDRA.*) Then yes, Alexandra, yes, I believe you are going to die.

He weeps.

I'm so sorry.

ALEXANDRA: I'm going to die.

DOCTOR: Yes.

ALEXANDRA: I'm going to die. I am going to die!

DOCTOR: Why does that make you happy? I don't understand.

ALEXANDRA: I am going to die!

DOCTOR: You're frightening me.

ALEXANDRA: Don't be frightened. Death is so much less terrible than life. Come here. Don't be frightened, dear doctor. I'm going to die. Now we know. And now at last I can tell you: I love you.

DOCTOR: Stop it. (*To TURGENEV.*) Never stop. Never ever.

ALEXANDRA: I love you, doctor.

DOCTOR: Tell me till the end of time! Alexandra Andreyevna loved me! (*To ALEXANDRA.*) But you can't love me. It's impossible. I have failed you. What is there to love?

ALEXANDRA: Come here.

She takes his head in her hands. She kisses him on the head. He whimpers. She tilts his head up and kisses him on the lips. He utters a small cry and lets his head sink down into the pillow. She now begins to cry. He now tries to comfort her.

I don't understand.

DOCTOR: Neither do I.

ALEXANDRA: Why are you so shy? Was I mistaken? Do you not love me after all? In which case, forgive me.

DOCTOR: No, I do love you. I love you so much my heart could burst!

ALEXANDRA: Then why did you pull away?

DOCTOR: Because it's all too sad. We'll never be able to have this love.

ALEXANDRA: We have it now!

DOCTOR: You're dying. It's too painful.

ALEXANDRA: But the love itself will live. In your memory. Hold me. Our love will be like an iridescent butterfly, a brief and joyous miracle. Don't cut its short life even shorter. Why will you not hold me?

DOCTOR: Why? (*To TURGENEV.*) Because I'm not a tall man. I have no 'breeding' to speak of. She was so beautiful and I'm a sort of stunted weasel, crossed with a bullfrog. She was so cultivated. She could have had her pick from the noblest men in Russia. Yes, I've cobbled together some learning, come away with some bits of paper, but I'm not widely read. I've forgotten my Latin. She was going to die at twenty without ever having loved, and that's what tormented her, and that's why, in despair, she seized on me. (*To ALEXANDRA.*) Have pity on me, Alexandra. Have pity on us both.

ALEXANDRA: What is there to pity? Don't you understand that I've got to die?

DOCTOR: Exactly.

ALEXANDRA: No, I have to die! I must die! Don't you see, there's no way back? Climb up on the bed!

DOCTOR: Alexandra.

ALEXANDRA: Hold me!

She pulls him closer to her, holding him tightly in her arms.

That's it. I love you, and you love me, and our love is all the sweeter because I shan't be here to see it fade. I have loved you, so now I have to die.

DOCTOR: No! I will cure you somehow! I'll send for help. The best doctors from Peter, Moscow, Paris, London. I will pay for them to come. I'll sell my house. I will cure you, and we will ask for your mother's blessing. Nothing will bring us asunder. We will be happy.

ALEXANDRA: You don't understand, my darling. If I were to live…if I were to hope for a long and respectable life…you must see that we…my father could never have countenanced such a…you wouldn't want me to be ashamed, would you? It would be far worse than death – look at you, you silly man – how could you and I…? Not in the real world. But still, here, in this room, we knew what it was to love and be loved, and it was beautiful, but now I have to die.

DOCTOR: Yes. Yes, of course.

ALEXANDRA: You told me I had to die. And you're the doctor.

Silence.

What is your Christian name?

DOCTOR: (*To TURGENEV.*) Why should I keep that a secret now? (*To ALEXANDRA.*) Trifon.

ALEXANDRA: What?

DOCTOR: Trifon. (*To TURGENEV.*) The reason I became a doctor, so I could at last be called something that didn't make people howl with scorn.

ALEXANDRA cannot help herself – she laughs, not uncruelly.

ALEXANDRA: Trifon! *Et il croyait que nous pouvons nous marier! Mon dieu! Trifon – mon amour! Mon amour, Trifon! Hahaha!*

DOCTOR: (*To TURGENEV.*) Well, that's about it. The priest came and went. She surprised us and hung on for another three days. By the end she was barely recognisable. I've seen prettier things laid out in a coffin. I don't know how I survived. The things she told me. Foul, unrepeatable things. Vulgarity spewing from every orifice. For God's sake, I thought, just put her out of her misery, but of course that's precisely what I was already doing. I was her misery. And she mine. The cause, the symptom – and the cure.

MOTHER: Doctor?

DOCTOR: Come in.

MOTHER: God protect her soul.

DOCTOR: I have to warn you, she's…

ALEXANDRA: Mother!

MOTHER: She knows me.

ALEXANDRA: Father! Hold father's hand, mother. I've something to announce. Trifon and I are going to be married. We're crazily in love.

DOCTOR: It's the fever.

ALEXANDRA: He has a ridiculous name but he's fantastic in bed! He's like a rapacious lion under the sheets. It's a bit early to tell, but you may want to start knitting some bootees. You'll be fabulous grandparents. You do approve? Well, we couldn't care less if you do or not, could we Trifon?

DOCTOR: She's delirious.

ALEXANDRA: We've exchanged rings. You've had my ring a number of times, haven't you, Treefy? Don't blush. He's insatiable. He's literally loved the living daylights out of me. No, but my little gold one that you gave me, father. Show them the ring, Trifon!

DOCTOR: What ring?

ALEXANDRA: Give me your hand.

DOCTOR: I've got to get some air.

MOTHER: It's all right, doctor. Really, it's all right.

DOCTOR: (*To TURGENEV.*) And it was. She died the next day. A huge relief for everyone. I had been in that room for ten days and yet it felt like ten years. Just before she died she asked to speak to me alone.

ALEXANDRA: Perhaps I've acted wrongly towards to you. Forgive me. It's my illness.

DOCTOR: (*To TURGENEV.*) How we use our illness to excuse. Are we afraid of being well, do you think? In case it brings happiness? And that would never do.

ALEXANDRA: It made me say some terrible things, but believe me, I've never loved anyone more than you.

36

DOCTOR: (*To TURGENEV.*) What did that mean?

ALEXANDRA: Don't forget me. Treasure my ring.

DOCTOR: Never loved anyone more than me.

ALEXANDRA: Hold me. Hold me, Trifon.

He does so. She breathes her last. After a while, he covers her and walks away. The MOTHER holds out a fifty rouble note.

MOTHER: The coachman's here. I'd like you to have this, as a token of my gratitude. You did your best.

DOCTOR: I did...all I could. (*To TURGENEV.*) No other doctor would have...could have done... I refused to take the money.

MOTHER: Please come to the funeral. You knew her.

DOCTOR: Yes, of course.

MOTHER: Thank you, doctor. And you can keep the ring.

DOCTOR: I don't know what you're...

She and the daughter disappear. The DOCTOR takes a small ring out of his pocket and puts it on his pinkie.

(*To TURGENEV.*) I've never worn it. In case it makes her jealous. Yes, I've since got myself a wife. Gone in for holy matrimony, as they call it. Spiteful bitch, ugly as sin, but at least her name is no less ridiculous than mine. Akulina. Merchant's daughter, thick as shit, wouldn't know a book if it dropped on her head. She's like a grub. Sleeps all day. Only wakes up to feed her face. Only thing fatter than her is the dowry that came with her. Seven thousand juicy roubles. It's a question of finding your level. I did enjoy that game of cards. I might wear this now. Sod the wife. Listen, what I said about scatterguns...oh, never mind. I'll call by tomorrow morning – if you're still with us, that is. Yes, a pretty ring. It'll be a reminder. To observe the golden rule: never get involved. Looks like rain again. Lucky I enjoy a nice walk.

He leaves. TURGENEV reaches into his pocket and pulls out a notebook and pencil. He begins to write. The MAID enters to take away the tea-things. He looks up. She looks at him. They hold each other's gaze. She smiles seductively, coyly, then leaves. He carries on writing. The lights fade.

*